Write Freely: Kick Start Your Writing

Scott P. Craig

Dedication

First and foremost, I must thank God.

Michelle, this book would not have been possible without your love, guidance, and support. You are my inspiration.

This book is also dedicated to my father who helped edit and format this manuscript.

Contents

Introduction

Who among us has not sat staring blankly as you search mind thinking of something to write? Your frustration grows as you try to get past writer's block. You are stuck and need help. There is, however, a solution: freewriting.

Freewriting frees you from blank stares, empty thoughts, procrastination, and inhabitations. Here is how freewriting works:

- First, you are given a prompt about which to write.

- Second, you are given **five minutes** to write each prompt.

- Finally, you are free to write as you see fit with no requirements on style, grammar, length etc. Thoughts flow more freely, new ideas are generated, and you are able to move past writer's block with freewriting. Freewriting warms up the mind and prepares it to write.

Write Freely: Kick Start Your Writing will free you from your literary slump. This book offers a fresh, unique approach to freewriting. The prompts are novel, interesting, and guaranteed to bring any writer out of his or her writer's block. Little outside knowledge is required to complete the prompts. All you need is a good imagination and a desire to write freely.

With over 600 writing prompts, *Write Freely* is the most versatile and voluminous tool to quickly end writer's block and spur creativity for any writer.

Now, begin your journey and write freely.

A Day in the Life of ...

Discuss what an average day is like for these people. Be vivid and imaginative. (You can write these in narrative form.)

1. Oprah Winfrey.

2. A teenage boy uncertain of his sexual orientation.

3. Frank Sinatra.

4. Young ice skater training for the Olympics.

5. Al Capone.

6. Contestant on *American Idol*.

7. A 13-year-old South African girl infected with AIDS.

8. A beginning writer.

9. Jesus as a young boy.

10. Your next-door neighbor.

Add and See

Below a person is placed in an unusual scenario. Be very imaginative with what you feel would happen in that scenario.

1. Add Sarah Palin to a dinner hosted by Barack Obama.

2. Add a disorderly derelict to a high society fundraiser for the homeless.

3. Add a spiked punch bowl to an A.A. meeting.

4. Add an atheist to the Last Supper.

5. Add an inner city teenager to a wealthy, upper crust family.

6. Add a joyous event to the life of the most miserable person you know.

7. Add yourself to a dinner with one of your heroes.

8. Add Michael Moore to a cross-country road trip with George W. Bush.

9. Add a change in gender to your spouse.

10. Add a clown to your son's 18th birthday party.

Advice Column

Answer the following questions as an advice columnist. Give yourself a handle, be creative, and write in the voice of the columnist you create.

1. My 9-year-old son still sneaks into our bedroom at night. We put him out but he comes back in during the middle of the night. What should we do? *Signed: Rest in Peace.*

2. I walked in on my son smoking weed. I raised him not to do drugs. He doesn't know that I used to do drugs when I was young. Should I tell him so he doesn't go down my path or keep it to myself? *Signed: Smoke and Tell.*

3. After ten years of marriage, my husband won't kiss me. He says he doesn't like to kiss. I've never had any complaints in the past, so I think he just doesn't love me anymore. Am I wrong to feel this way? *Signed: Never been Kissed.*

4. My wife recently revealed that she is gay. I pleaded with her not to leave me, so she gave our marriage a second chance. Now, she stays out late with her best friend and sometimes doesn't come home. I'm scared to ask, but is my wife having an affair? *Signed: Scared Straight.*

5. I have been abused, cheated on, and neglected by men. "Mike" is unlike any man I have dated. He swept me off my feet. Last week, he asked me to marry him. I told him I needed time. I don't deserve such a wonderful man. What should I tell him? *Signed: Post Dated Love.*

6. My sister and I disagree on how to raise children. She spanks her boys and I use time outs. Her kids are better behaved, but not as happy as mine. So, who's right on the spanking issue? *Signed: To Spank or not to Spank.*

7. A fellow coworker steals lunches from the company refrigerator. I don't pack a lunch, so it doesn't affect me. Should I say something? I don't want to be the company snitch. *Signed: Company Coward.*

8. I have a problem telling the truth. I love to make up stories about anything that will make me look better. When I get caught, I lie to get out of previous lies. I'm not sure what the truth is these days. I need help. *Signed: Liar, Liar.*

9. My wife has a bad habit that I can't stand. She clips her toenails in bed. When I ask her not to do it, she says she cleans up after herself so it's not a problem. How do I get her to stop? *Signed: In a Toe Jam.*

10. One night I saw the neighbor across the way take his next-door neighbor's newspaper. An hour later he put it back on his neighbor's porch. I feel he took the paper without permission, so I watched the next morning, and I saw the same thing. Should I say something? *Signed: Paper Peeper.*

The Best and Worst

In this section, select one choice and write about it.

1. Describe your **(best/worst)** friend.

2. What was your **(best/worst)** date like?

3. Write about your **(best/worst)** holiday experience.

4. Write about the **(best/worst)** thing you have ever done to someone.

5. Discuss your **(best/worst)** childhood memory.

6. Describe your **(best/worst)** job.

7. Describe your **(best/worst)** girlfriend or boyfriend.

8. Discuss the **(best/worst)** car you have ever owned.

9. Who was the **(best/worst)** President of the United States?

10. Describe the **(best/worst)** secret you were asked to keep.

Cause and Effect

Decisions impact us in so many ways - some good, some bad, and a whole lot in-between. Take these various issues and describe the impact that making these decisions can have on you and your community.

1. Drinking and driving.

2. Unprotected sex.

3. Starting a war.

4. Spanking a child.

5. Placing an embargo on a country.

6. Giving a child up for adoption.

7. Providing drug addicts with clean needles.

8. Telling white lies.

9. Forgiving someone who has harmed you.

10. Having an affair.

Challenging Prompts

Take the opposing view from your personal beliefs on the following issues and people. As a writer, you must understand a story from every angle.

1. Abortion.

2. America.

3. Your family.

4. Religion.

5. Death penalty.

6. Integration.

7. War.

8. Universal health care.

9. Registering sex offenders.

10. Welfare.

Children's Stories

Construct a children's story around the facts and characters given below.

1. Nate and C.J. were playing in their family's attic when they happened upon a bottle marked, "DO NOT USE." Their curiosity overcame them and they sprayed the clear liquid.

2. An impish little boy happens upon a squirrel that has learned to talk.

3. Mr. Fuzzy is a hippopotamus that lives in a zoo. After closing, he sets himself and the other animals free.

4. Elaine, a shy little girl, finds some magical tap shoes while walking home from school.

5. Rebekah wanted nothing more in life than to take dance lessons. She and her mother walked past a dance studio.

6. Rosario and Hector played in the woods behind their home. They went deeper than they ever had been and came across an opening to a cave.

7. Marvin is a blind boy who loves to play the piano.

8. Martian siblings, Xertas and Yerf, longed to see other worlds.

9. Jeremiah and Stacy find a glowing box in the woods.

10. One morning before school started, Dee discovered she can read people's minds.

Clichés

Write a story based on the following clichés:

1. Read between the lines.

2. You can never go home again.

3. Has an ax to grind.

4. Take it with a grain of salt.

5. That takes the cake.

6. Scared of his own shadow.

7. Silence is golden.

8. Every dog has its day.

9. You can lead a horse to water, but you can't make him drink.

10. Glutton for punishment.

Compare and Contrast

You are given two subjects to compare and contrast. Be descriptive and creative. (You may wish to write a story pitting the two subjects against one another.)

1. Your mom & your dad.

2. Your life during high school & after high school.

3. Wal-Mart & Mom and Pop stores.

4. Funerals & Weddings.

5. America today & America 50 years ago.

6. Hope & Faith.

7. Quality & Quantity.

8. Urban & Rural lifestyles.

9. Soldiers & Protestors.

10. Writing for money & Writing for pleasure.

Creative Writing Prompts

Create a story around the following scenarios.

1. Divorced mother, dating again, three kids, on her first date in 12 years.

2. A man meets the woman of his dreams but his family wants nothing to do with her.

3. Cheryl tests her sobriety as she tries to come to terms with her daughter's untimely death.

4. Freed from cancer, Marlo is determined to embark on a new life.

5. Two sisters discover that they are in love with the same man. They confront him to get him to choose one of them.

6. It is 1492 and two small children are playing along the shores of the ocean when they see an odd ship sailing towards them.

7. Walking in the woods, a man sees the corner of a box sticking out of freshly disturbed soil.

8. The newest teller of a bank is startled to see a man wanted for armed robbery enter the bank.

9. Deciding to free himself from the bondage of slavery, Elijah manages to escape.

10. An aspiring writer goes to his first writer's conference and bumps into his literary hero.

Crime and Criminal Justice

1. Can crime ever be justified? If so, when, why, and how?

2. Is there such a thing as a victimless crime – such as drugs and gambling?

3. Are having cameras throughout a city a good or bad idea?

4. If you could get away with it, what crime would you commit and why?

5. If a person gets into a barroom brawl and kills the person he was fighting, should he face the death penalty?

6. Defend the maxim, "An eye for an eye."

7. How can a person succeed in life after being released from prison?

8. Write about an unemployed man's descent into a criminal life.

9. Should we jail criminals to reform them, punish them, or keep them off the streets?

10. What are the ramifications of legalizing marijuana?

Dates and Dating

1. Describe your first date.

2. How long should someone date before proposing marriage and why?

3. Discuss the details of one of your blind dates.

4. Make the case that men should pay on the first date.

5. What would you do on a date if you only had $40?

6. With an unlimited budget, describe your dream date.

7. Discuss how a lack of physical attraction can be overcome by a few good dates.

8. Is dating easier today or more difficult?

9. Write about your parents' first date.

10. Create a story about a date where something shocking is revealed.

Death

Write the eulogies for the people listed below. Be creative and feel free to embellish to make your story more dynamic.

1. Your mother.

2. A sibling.

3. Your best friend.

4. Your significant other.

5. The last person you saw in person.

6. Tom Cruise.

7. Your father.

8. Mark Twain.

9. Your hero.

10. Darth Vader.

Deserted Island Scenario

Describe life on a deserted island with the following people or things:

1. An old high school crush.

2. Your mother.

3. Inflatable raft with a hole in it.

4. Your pet.

5. A heroin addict going through withdrawals.

6. A small infant.

7. Snooki.

8. A grown man with childlike intelligence.

9. Two weeks worth of food.

10. Your worst enemy.

Dialogue

Use the dialogue below to complete the story. Take the story in whatever direction you wish. Have fun with this one.

1. "Jerry, I can't continue to do this anymore," Amy said in an exhausted tone.

2. Mrs. Rodriguez reared back and said, "I'm happily married."

3. "You know," said Bill, "I've never heard you talk about Dad before."

4. With tears in her eyes Jasmine asked, "Where do we go from here?"

5. "Hector, you know better than anyone that we can't possibly do that."

6. "Stop," Meredith ordered, "or we won't be able to go back."

7. All alone, Lucy cried, "Why is this happening to me?"

8. As they went further down into the basement, they heard a voice say, "Stop."

9. "Mommy, wipe your eyes. It'll be okay."

10. "Don't be so dense John, your mother has hated you since the day you were born," Polly barked.

Dilemmas

Write what you would do in the following situations.

1. You hold the arms of your two children, but only have enough strength to hold onto one as they hang off the edge of a cliff. What do you do?

2. You are in a small plane with one other passenger. The plane is crashing with only one parachute. What do you do?

3. Your daughter is addicted to heroin and sells her body to buy heroin. Do you allow her to continue to sell her body, or do you buy it for her so she can avoid selling her body and all the risks that come with that?

4. You discover your brother's wife is having an affair. Telling him would devastate him, split the family, and possibly ruin your relationship. What would you do?

5. Gang members have moved into a house in your neighborhood and are selling drugs out of the house. Reporting them could lead to serious retaliation for you and your neighbors. What do you do?

6. You and your best friend are arrested for burglary. If you place the blame on him, you get probation. If you say nothing, you may get a full prison sentence. The same applies to your friend. What do you do and why?

7. While at the beach, you see a small child who appears to be drowning. No one is within earshot and she is going to drown if someone does not help. You cannot swim and are afraid of the water. What do you do?

8. Your son is addicted to drugs so you decide to participate in an intervention to confront him with his problem. The intervention leader says that if your son says "no" to going to rehab, you must be willing to turn your back on him indefinitely. What do you do?

9. You sell you first novel, an autobiography, achieving a life long dream. The publisher wants you to embellish some facts to make your family seem dysfunctional and make the novel more sensational. What do you do?

10. Your eight-year-old niece tells you that her father, your brother, is touching her inappropriately. This seems so uncharacteristic of your brother and you worry about confronting him. What do you do?

Dreams

1. As a child, you and your best friend wander off into the woods around dusk. You come upon an abandoned shack. Complete the dream.

2. Use the third person to tell the story of the best dream you ever had.

3. Describe a reoccurring dream that you have.

4. What one dream would you be afraid to let anyone know about?

5. Discuss a dream a serial killer might have.

6. Create a story about a child who turns to her parents after a bad dream.

7. Tell the story of a man tortured by all of his dreams coming true.

8. Interpret your most recent dream.

9. Write about your most recent nightmare.

10. Create a story around a child who can enter people's dreams.

Emotions

1. Discuss a time you had conflicting emotions?

2. Describe the saddest moment in your life.

3. Describe the happiest moment in your life.

4. What is love?

5. Write a story that embodies the importance of hope.

6. How has anger hurt your life?

7. Tell a story of a post-partum depressed mother.

8. Create a story with a character that suffers from severe mood swings.

9. Describe what heartache feels like to someone who has never felt it?

10. Discuss a time you felt shame and why.

Ethical Issues

1. Imagine yourself as a criminal defense attorney. Your newest client tells you that she murdered her husband, but wants to plead not guilty. How do you in good conscience defend her?

2. You are a scientist who comes across a study that would cure cancer. The study came from experiments inflicted upon victims in Nazi concentration camps. What should you do?

3. You are a journalist who receives a juicy tip from a Washington insider. You promised not to reveal his identity. After the story breaks, you are brought up before an ethics panel to reveal your source or face jail. What should you do?

4. You do the bookkeeping for your church. You discover that the pastor is siphoning funds from the collection. It is not a lot of money. Revealing the theft will cause the church to splinter and ultimately die. What should you do?

5. A hurricane has devastated your town. You are a struggling contractor who found out that other contractors are adding 20% to their estimates to take advantage of the government money. Raising your bid 20% would allow you to hire workers you had to lay off. What should you do?

6. As a high school teacher, you add up the grades and discover that Emily will not graduate because she failed by one point. It is too late for extra credit. She will be the first in her family to go to college. No one will know if you raise her grade. What should you do?

7. In the middle of a college final exam, you innocently glance over at the paper of a student in front of you. She has correctly answered a question you passed previously because you did not know the answer. Do you use the answer you saw or skip it since you truly did not know the answer?

8. You recently diagnosed one of your patients with HIV. You tell him to tell his wife, but he refuses. The next day his wife comes in for an annual exam. You suggest an HIV/AIDS test. She refuses. She is upset that you insist and is about to leave. What should you do?

9. You are walking by an alley and come across a bag with $5,000. There is no one around. You can keep the money, turn it over to the police, or walk away from it. Pick one and defend your decision.

10. A young college professor meets an attractive young woman at a bar. He takes her home and they spend the evening together. The next morning he sees her in his 8 AM lecture that morning. Professors are forbidden from dating students. What should he do?

Ethnic and Minority Groups

This section asks questions that may be difficult to answer truthfully, but remember to be honest.

1. Describe a time when you felt discriminated against.

2. Write about a moment in your life when you knew that prejudice existed.

3. Describe the status of race relations in America.

4. Imagine yourself walking into a social situation where no one looks like you. Describe how you feel and how the people perceive you.

5. Describe a time when you heard a friend or family member make a derogatory remark about another ethnic or racial group and how it made you feel?

6. Write a story about a friend overhearing you make derogatory remarks about her race.

7. Find a stereotype you believe to be true and defend its validity.

8. Pick a different race from yourself and imagine being involved in a marriage to someone from that group. How would your life be different?

9. Discuss whether being in an interracial marriage ensures that a couple is free from prejudice?

10. Why do humans divide themselves along racial lines?

The Facts of Life

Write a story surrounding these facts. Be as creative as you wish.

1. May 29, 1953, John Hunt climbs to the summit of Mount Everest.

2. Stock Market Crash of 1929.

3. April 18, 1906, a major earthquake kills hundreds and destroys property in San Francisco.

4. March 6, 1836, The Alamo falls to the Mexicans led by General Santa Anna.

5. Roger Bannister runs the first mile under five minutes on May 6, 1954.

6. The Japanese attack Pearl Harbor on December 7, 1941.

7. On November 9, 1989, East Germans begin tearing down the Berlin Wall.

8. The bubonic plague ravishes Europe from 1347-1351.

9. Magic Johnson announces he has HIV in the fall of 1991.

10. December 2003, U.S. forces find Saddam Hussein hiding in a spider hole.

Family Life

1. What was your family life like growing up?

2. Discuss the pros and cons of adoption.

3. What is essential to have a great childhood and why?

4. Tell the story of a same sex couple seeking to adopt.

5. What beliefs or customs did you learn growing up?

6. Describe what it takes to be a good parent.

7. Discuss a time you felt you failed as a parent.

8. Discuss a time you have failed as a son/daughter.

9. Write a story of a child with a very dysfunctional family.

10. What impact does a single parent household have on children?

Famous & Infamous

Use your imagination and write about the following people, places, things, and events. You can write factually or invent scenarios involving them.

1. C.S. Lewis.

2. Hurricane Katrina - New Orleans.

3. Sarah Palin.

4. Jesse Owens at the 1936 Olympics.

5. The first Thanksgiving in the New World.

6. Cesar Chavez.

7. St. Valentine's Day Massacre.

8. Creation of the atomic bomb.

9. Raid on Osama bin Laden's compound.

10. Nelson Mandela.

Fantasy

Create fantasy stories based on the scenarios below.

1. A boy blows out his candles and his wish is granted upon opening his eyes.

2. Struggling to regain his balance, Mali finds himself before a two-headed figure, Blirton.

3. Romulo eagerly lapped up every drop of water from the bubbling spring. Instantly, he felt the difference.

4. In 16th century Europe, Camilia's brother takes a sip from the well and is immediately whisked away.

5. Morgan faces the first of three tasks he must complete to win the hand of Princess Tumia.

6. Xerhis has seconds to decide whether to eat Lilac of Covington or seize the Amulet of Phoriat.

7. Without warning, Polly ran in terror, leaving behind her friend. Beth stood as the rustling in the bushes grew closer.

8. "Take two drops and you'll be invisible," the old sorcerer told Grumblin. Grumblin went forth to his destiny.

9. Armida reads the plaque that states, "Bad luck will befall those who abuse the Cloak of Narcia."

10. Mike ate the forbidden berries that promised eternal youth and instantly knew the repercussions.

First Sentence

You are given the first line of a story. Write the remainder of the story.

1. This was the darkest time of my life.

2. Megan knew she had gone too far this time.

3. Jackson and Malcolm left Biloxi to start a new life together.

4. "Where were you last night?" she asked.

5. Freshly baked apple pies rested on everyone's windowsills that 4th of July.

6. Little did they know that this would be her last birthday alive.

7. "What should I tell her?" Mr. Gray asked.

8. She left the library, as she did every Friday night, and went home to look after her three cats.

9. Life had always been kind to Richard.

10. The Peace Corps offered him a chance at a new life.

The Five Senses

Close your eyes and imagine the impact of the item on your senses. Open your eyes and begin writing.

1. Hearing – A swarm of bees.

2. Hearing – A silent room.

3. Taste – Crepe paper.

4. Touch – An oyster.

5. Smell – Hanging laundry.

6. Taste & Smell – Cinnamon rolls.

7. Hearing & Sight – A quarreling couple.

8. Taste, Touch, & Sight – An ocean wave.

9. Smell, Taste, & Touch – Blueberry muffin.

10. Taste, Smell, Sight, & Touch – Butter.

Friends and Friendship

1. Tell a story of a woman who contemplates adding someone on Facebook.

2. What does your best friend mean to you? Write a letter to him/her.

3. Write a story about two best friends who end their friendship over a man.

4. What is the worst thing a friend has ever done to you?

5. What is the best thing a friend has ever done for you?

6. When was a time that you needed a friend the most?

7. Discuss a time you and a friend were in a petty fight.

8. How would you feel if your best friend revealed your secrets to your family?

9. What makes you a good a friend?

10. What childhood friend would you like to see again and why?

Gender Issues

1. Write a story involving the glass ceiling.

2. Defend the merits of women working outside the home.

3. How has the Women's Movement impacted your life?

4. Which parent is more important in your life and why?

5. How are men and women equal and unequal?

6. What one thing do you wish you could do that defies gender roles?

7. How are gender roles prevalent in same-sex relationships?

8. Are women or men better writers? Cite examples.

9. Which woman shattered gender roles in a way no one had done previously?

10. How do gender roles vary by ethnic and minority groups?

Good vs. Evil

Discuss the battle or feud between the following factions.

1. Democrats vs. Republicans.

2. God vs. The Devil.

3. Israelis vs. Palestinians.

4. Axis Power vs. Allied Power.

5. The North vs. The South.

6. Rich vs. Poor.

7. Muslims vs. The West.

8. Capitalists vs. Socialists.

9. Management vs. Labor.

10. North Korea vs. South Korea.

Healing

1. Who do you need to forgive and why?

2. Write a story of a man who has forgiven the father that beat him as a child.

3. Discuss a situation that required you to seek someone else's forgiveness.

4. Tell the story of a woman who seeks the man who raped her to tell him she forgives him.

5. How has seeking revenge backfired on you?

6. Write a letter designed to bring about peace between Palestinians and Israelis.

7. If you could mediate a dispute between two parties, who would it be and why?

8. Is forgiveness a two-way street or can a person do it without the other?

9. Write a letter to someone who hurt you.

10. Write a letter to someone you have hurt.

History

1. Discuss the single most important historic event?

2. Which society had the greatest impact on modern civilization and why?

3. Write the biography of a significant historical figure.

4. Write the story of the colonialization of America.

5. If you could visit any time period, which would it be and why?

6. If you could meet any person from history, who would it be and why?

7. Which war most impacted the world and why?

8. Which person most impacted the world and why?

9. Why should Native Americans be granted land as reparations?

10. Write the history of the world since your birth.

Holidays

1. Why are many people sad during the holidays?

2. Write a story about your most recent Thanksgiving.

3. Discuss why Santa Claus should be removed from public schools.

4. Make the case for a holiday we should celebrate but do not.

5. Why should stores be closed for Christmas and Thanksgiving?

6. Write about your worst holiday experience.

7. Explain Thanksgiving to someone from another country.

8. Create a story about an American family celebrating the 4th of July overseas.

9. Tell someone unfamiliar with Yom Kippur about it.

10. Describe your worst birthday and why it was so bad.

Hopes, Dreams, and Wishes

1. Discuss whether dreams can ever be too lofty.

2. Write a letter to your child(ren) with all the words of wisdom they will need to guide them.

3. Describe a dream that came true and how you felt.

4. Write about a dream you want to fulfill and the steps necessary to reach it.

5. What would you wish for if you were granted one wish?

6. Write about someone whose dream has changed the world.

7. When have you allowed fear to keep you from keeping your hope alive?

8. Why do some people feel the need to dash other people's dreams?

9. Write a poem about what hope means.

10. Write about your hopes, dreams, and wishes for your writing.

Horror/Scary

Write a scary story around the facts given below.

1. A knock at the door sank his heart.

2. Desmond knew he could no longer run from his past.

3. Jack and Wanda knew nothing of their home's history.

4. The knife dripped with her mother's blood, as she stood motionless.

5. Greeted by a dead end as she turned the corner, her heart sank.

6. No one knew about Miguel's basement. That was about to end.

7. With each step, the doll's eyes eerily followed him.

8. Mercedes looked into her baby's eyes and knew something was wrong.

9. IIe looked at her smile and felt at ease. He foolishly trusted his instincts.

10. Cat and Mary chased their new classmate into the old abandoned house.

How Do You...

1. How do you ensure that your marriage is successful?

2. How do you sell your book to a literary agent?

3. How do you get away with a crime?

4. How do you change a tire?

5. How do you escape from the pain in your life?

6. How do you justify your stance on religion?

7. How do you cook your favorite meal?

8. How do you get someone to fall in love with you?

9. How do you break bad news to someone?

10. How do you decide when to trust your instincts?

Inspiration

1. Where do you find the inspiration to write?

2. Write about a person who inspires you to be better.

3. Find inspiration in a book and write about it.

4. How do children inspire you?

5. Write a story about a fictional inspirational character.

6. Discuss your characteristics that inspire others.

7. Who is your hero and why?

8. Which author inspires your writing style and why?

9. What role does religion play in providing you with inspiration?

10. How do your parents inspire you?

Instructions

Write step-by-step instructions for the following:

1. Having an affair.

2. Raising a child.

3. Writing the Great American Novel.

4. Developing a great friendship.

5. Becoming a famous actor.

6. Solving a murder mystery.

7. Running for mayor.

8. Searching for a job.

9. Organizing a protest.

10. Bringing about world peace.

Journal

Complete the journal entry with what you feel comes next.

1. Last night he did it again. My tears mean nothing. My "no's" mean nothing. Maybe I mean nothing....

2. I will never understand love. Why do men seem to run from a good woman? I know I deserve better....

3. Mom and Dad can't seem to get it together. They fight like cats and dogs. I know it's going to happen. I just know it....

4. I know I need to tell her but I can't. How in the hell did I manage to fall in love with a man? I'm not gay. I can't be....

5. Arnold forgot my birthday again. I'm not sure why I've stayed with him so long....

6. AIDS, I can't believe I am going to die. I can't believe my life is over. What did I do to deserve this? If only....

7. Finally, it happened. I can't believe it. It was so amazing. I enjoyed unwrapping the mystery of it all....

8. Why do I fall for his promises? It's the same thing over and over again. "I promise I'll be there this time." Yeah right....

9. This has been the worst day of my life. I am so mortified. In front of everybody. They all laughed too....

10. Grandma and Pa-Pa still send me a kiddy card with $5. Hello, I'm 27 now! Their heart is in the right place, but I'm not that goofy little kid anymore....

Last Sentence

You are given the last sentence of a story. Write the story that precedes it.

1. Harry never looked back, for he was finally happy.

2. Huddled together for warmth, they saw the rope drop down for the last rescue.

3. They kissed, joined hands, and walked down the boardwalk one last time.

4. With Kansas City in Karen's rearview mirror, she gripped the wheel firmly, turned up the radio, and let her hair fall to her shoulders.

5. Marvin's Cafe was now a distant memory.

6. He got the last word in after all.

7. "Thanks Mom."

8. The girls now knew how their mother felt over 30 years ago.

9. As the flowers left his hand, a tear streamed down his cheek.

10. The shores of his native Brazil warmed his dying heart.

Letters

Write a love letter to the following:

1. Your significant other.

2. Your first boy/girlfriend.

3. A secret crush.

Write a tell-all letter revealing your deepest secret to the following:

4. Your significant other.

5. Your child(ren).

6. Your parents.

7. God.

Write letters to these (in)famous personalities:

8. O.J. Simpson.

9. Your congressman.

10. Justin Bieber.

Marriage and Marital Issues

1. What are the benefits of being married?

2. What should be the law regarding same-sex marriages?

3. What are the challenges facing an interracial marriage?

4. Tell the story of a couple marrying in Las Vegas.

5. What are the five most important issues a couple should discuss before marriage and why?

6. If you could do your wedding over again, what would you do differently?

7. Describe an ideal bachelor or bachelorette party.

8. Why is living together a viable alternative to marriage for so many couples today?

9. Write the wedding vows you would like to use at your wedding.

10. Describe your ideal wedding in great detail.

Mores and Folkways

Mores and folkways are customs and norms that are so engrained in society that they are not to be deviated from or violated.

1. Write a story where a woman commits a heinous taboo.

2. Discuss a time you broke a custom and the consequence of it.

3. Why does society forbid certain acts?

4. Create a story about a pair of teenagers who try to live as vampires.

5. Write a story about adultery.

6. Write a story about a teenage boy who violates gender roles.

7. Write a story about an employee's first day at a nudist colony.

8. Tell the story of a chronic thumb-sucking adult.

9. Why are people often attracted to that which is forbidden?

10. What societal rules should be changed or ended?

Mystery and Who Done Its

Write mystery stories based on the scenarios and facts listed below.

1. Write a Sherlock Holmes mystery set in modern times.

2. A woman, a missing daughter, a broken window, and a note.

3. Write a story of two children who solve a murder in their town.

4. Write a mystery set in the Old West.

5. Bloody knife, blood stained clothes, and a power outage.

6. Write a mystery set in Victorian England.

7. A watch, 2 sets of fingerprints, and an old deed.

8. Write the story of the world's first female sleuth.

9. Tire tracks, a letter opener, torn piece of fabric, and a missing diamond ring.

10. Write a story about a reluctant sleuth trying to find his missing wife.

Myth, Legend, and Folklore

1. Why were the stories of ancient mythology created?

2. Which superstitions do you observe and why?

3. Write a chain letter. (Please do not send it out.)

4. Tell the story of a mythological god.

5. Write a fairy tale with two small children and their father.

6. Create a bedtime story with a good and bad witch and a lesson to be learned.

7. Mythology was believed to be true in ancient times. Will there ever come a time when a modern religion will be looked upon as mere mythology?

8. Write your own version of an Aesop fable.

9. What is your favorite American folklore story and why?

10. How are women represented in ancient folklore?

Opinions

Write an op-ed piece on the following issues:

1. The latest political scandal.

2. Tax cuts.

3. The state of race relations in America today.

4. Reality television stars.

5. Leash laws.

6. Sex and violence in today's movies.

7. Separation of church and state.

8. Cloning

9. Global warming.

10. Global economy.

Philosophy

Create a story around these philosophical quotes.

1. "We are what we repeatedly do." Aristotle.

2. "I no longer want to walk on worn soles." Friedrich Nietzsche.

3. "Too many of us are not living our dreams, because we are living our fears." Les Brown.

4. "Happiness is a continuation of happenings which are not resisted." Deepak Chopra.

5. "No man's error becomes his own law; nor obliges him to persist in it." Thomas Hobbes.

6. "Better a diamond with a flaw than a pebble without." Confucius.

7. "From each according to his abilities, to each according to his needs." Karl Marx.

8. "I have always thought the actions of men the best interpreters of their thoughts." John Locke.

9. "Only the dead have seen the end of the war." Plato.

10. "A man who carries a cat by the tail learns something he can learn in no other way." Mark Twain.

Phobias and Fears

Write a story involving each phobia listed below. Have your character face his/her phobia, whether he/she conquers it or not.

1. Isolophobia - Fear of being alone or solitude.

2. Agoraphobia - Fear of crowded public places like markets.

3. Myctophobia - Fear of darkness.

4. Oneirophobia - Fear of dreams.

5. Mysophobia - Fear of being contaminated with germs.

6. Geliophobia - Fear of laughter.

7. Androphobia - Fear of men.

8. Peccatophobia - Fear of sinning.

9. Kenophobia - Fear of empty spaces.

10. Chiraptophobia - Fear of being touched.

Poem Prompts

Here you are given the first or last two lines of a poem. Complete the missing part.

1. For each moment together. Eyes unite and stares smolder...

2. ...Motion is slowed to a dizzying pace. Heed the calls and admonishments.

3. Mama, you loved me when the world didn't. You are the reason why we sing...

4. ...Your heart is cold and dead. Yet, I can't get the image of you from my head.

5. Smash against the rocks, let the crest rise. The rocks hold steady against your relentless assault...

6. ...The buzz grows louder with each passing. From a hum to a hiss.

7. Boom, crank, whack, smack. The machine turns and out pours the workers for the daily grind...

8. ...Pretentiously free. No need to worry, it's all about me.

9. Where are we now and where are we to go? The cold damp memories of you fade which each passing day...

10. ...Silently, the sun warms. Steady must we be.

Political

1. Discuss the greatest political challenge today?

2. Why do politics and corruption often find themselves intertwined?

3. What do you look for in a political leader?

4. Tell the story of a political revolutionary.

5. Discuss why many people follow political parties.

6. Discuss the reasons why you do or do not vote.

7. Describe the greatest political leader.

8. Why should corporations be allowed to donate money to campaigns?

9. What obstacles do women face in politics?

10. Make the case for or against term limits.

Pros and Cons

Weigh the pros and cons of the subject offered.

1. Nuclear energy.

2. Freedom of speech.

3. War.

4. Abortion.

5. Gun rights.

6. Gay rights.

7. Capitalism.

8. Religion.

9. Divorce.

10. Patriot Act.

Proverbs

Write a story that involves a proverb below without quoting it in the story.

1. No man can serve two masters.

2. Do not wear out your welcome.

3. Opportunity seldom knocks twice.

4. As you sow, so shall you reap.

5. Good fences make good neighbors.

6. The love of money is the root of all evil.

7. Experience is the best teacher.

8. They that dance must pay the fiddler.

9. Two is company, three is a crowd.

10. He that knows nothing, doubts nothing.

Quote-Based Prompts

Read the following quotes and write what comes to mind.

1. "He that is of the opinion money will do everything may well be suspected of doing everything for money." Benjamin Franklin.

2. "The weak can never forgive. Forgiveness is the attribute of the strong." Mahatma Gandhi.

3. "Although the world is full of suffering, it is full also of the overcoming of it." Helen Keller.

4. "A woman is like a tea bag - you never know how strong she is until she gets in hot water." Eleanor Roosevelt.

5. "In the end, we will remember not the words of our enemies, but the silence of our friends." The Rev. Martin Luther King, Jr.

6. "War may sometimes be a necessary evil. But no matter how necessary, it is always an evil, never a good." Jimmy Carter.

7. "Teachers open the door. You enter by yourself." Chinese Proverb.

8. "Seduction is enticing someone into doing what they secretly want to do already." Waiter Rant.

9. "A successful marriage is an edifice that must be rebuilt every day." Andre Maurois.

10. "Inches make a champion." Vince Lombardi.

Religion & Spirituality

1. Karl Marx once said, "Religion is the opiate for the masses." Explain why he is either right or wrong.

2. Why do or do you not believe in God?

3. How has prayer helped you?

4. Why do some abandon faith when a prayer goes unanswered?

5. If you were not your current religion, which would you choose and why?

6. Why do you or do you not attend church?

7. Create a story of Muslim living in Israel.

8. What qualities does it take to lead a church?

9. Discuss whether a church should perform same-sex marriages.

10. Describe what is lacking in today's churches.

Secrets

1. What is your biggest secret and why will you not tell it?

2. Describe a devastating secret a friend has told you.

3. If you have told someone's secret, what was it and what was the outcome?

4. Many families have secrets. What is your family secret or what do you suspect is a secret within your family?

5. Create a story about a man who hides something quite painful from others.

6. Write a story about a friend betraying a friend by revealing her secret and the consequence that unfolds.

7. What secret do you think the government is keeping from its citizens and why?

8. Write a story about a woman living with a secret and how it impacts her relationships.

9. Why do so many people eventually reveal their secret in some form or another?

10. If you had an affair, who would you tell and why?

Short Story Prompts

Write a story based on the scenarios below.

1. A small Midwestern town has its first murder in over fifty years. An FBI agent from Chicago comes to investigate.

2. Two best friends embark on a road trip to Hollywood. Both dream of acting, but only one will make it.

3. A Milwaukee factory worker meets the man of her dreams. They plan a wedding, but soon a problem emerges.

4. Leaving to pursue his dream, Devon struggles with guilt and returns after failing to achieve his dream.

5. A man sacrifices his life to take care of his wife after she is debilitated by a massive stroke.

6. After losing his job, 28-year-old Mark Weinstein moves in with his parents. He now struggles to regain his footing.

7. Lucy struggles to make ends meet for herself and her nine year old daughter. She comes across an ad for a job that will change her life forever.

8. Jackson travels to his ancestral lands on the Oneida reservation to connect with his father's family.

9. Jason and Lamont, two college students, spend Thanksgiving with their roommate's dysfunctional family.

10. Samantha, a nine year old, works to overcome her disability despite her mother's lack of support.

Social Problems & Contemporary Issues

1. Discuss whether poverty is a symptom of nature, nurture, or even both.

2. How do you solve racism?

3. How do you solve the famines throughout Africa?

4. Defend someone's right to bear arms.

5. Why should cigarettes be made illegal?

6. How would you solve the issue of obesity in children?

7. How has modern music become too explicit?

8. Defend the practice of outsourcing jobs overseas.

9. Discuss whether nuclear weapons more dangerous in the hands of rogue nations (e.g., North Korea) or superpowers (e.g., United States)?

10. Defend employers' right to charge more for health care for obese employees.

Telephone

Create a mock telephone conversation between the two people listed below. Use this exercise to work on dialogue.

1. President George W. Bush & President Barack Obama.

2. Your mother and you.

3. Bill Gates & the poorest person in the world.

4. An atheist & God.

5. Casey Anthony and an outraged citizen.

6. A man and a woman, who have met online, but have yet to meet in person.

7. A pastor and his mistress.

8. Military officer calling the mother of a fallen solider.

9. Son calling his mother and father to tell them about the newest edition to the family.

10. Literary agent calling an author to tell her that her book will be published.

Time

1. Discuss something you want to see happen in your future.

2. Describe one thing you regret not doing in your past.

3. Time heals all wounds. Tell the story of a time this occurred in your life.

4. Write your obituary.

5. Write a story about the past repeating itself and how the main character did not learn from a previous mistake.

6. Pretend you fell into a deep sleep and woke 100 years from now. Describe the awakening and your new life and surroundings.

7. Compare your personality today to how you were as a child.

8. Write a story where an event in a woman's life impacts her ten years later.

9. Write a poem about time.

10. Tell the story of your family's history up until your birth.

Time Travel

Go back in time to the events below and write what you think it was like to witness or live through these events.

1. East Berliner tearing down the Berlin Wall.

2. Office worker escaping the World Trade Center after a plane crashed into it.

3. Witness your birth through the eyes of your father.

4. Roman soldier marching alongside Jesus as he carries the cross on his back.

5. Father who leads his family westward after the Civil War.

6. Child watching her parents struggle during the Great Depression.

7. The first woman to write a book.

8. Ann Frank as she and her family go into hiding.

9. Hearing the Rev. Martin Luther King's, "I Have a Dream" speech.

10. Princess Diana being chased by paparazzi in France.

War and Peace

1. Write about the Civil War from a Confederate soldier's perspective.

2. Throughout history, why has peace been so hard to attain?

3. What does it take to win a war?

4. Who is the greatest peacemaker and why?

5. Write a story about a president who struggles emotionally with going to war.

6. What can you do to bring about peace in your community?

7. Write about the emotions of holding your best friend as he dies in your arms.

8. Can love truly conquer all? Explain.

9. Why should losing nations be required to pay war reparations?

10. Write a speech for Cindy Shcchan, who became an activist against the Iraq war after her son was killed in combat.

What if ...

1. You were a different gender?

2. You could be invisible for a day?

3. You were God?

4. You had everything you wanted in life?

5. You sold your novel?

6. You could read people's minds?

7. You were famous?

8. You lived in a war torn nation?

9. You knew you were going to die tomorrow?

10. You witnessed a murder?

Word Association

Provide the first word that comes to mind when you read the words below. Then write a story involving the two words.

1. Immediate.

2. Solitude.

3. Placate.

4. Verbose.

5. Phony.

6. Jubilant.

7. Abandon.

8. Pretentious.

9. Picturesque.

10. Complacent.

Word of the Day

Create a story around each word.

1. Hopeless.

2. Glutton.

3. Mystical.

4. Deference.

5. Relentless.

6. Unavailable.

7. Apathy.

8. Unrequited.

9. Abundance.

10. Jubilant.

Writing

1. Why do you write?

2. What is your dream writing assignment and why?

3. Describe how you felt when you first got published?

4. Create a story about an unsuccessful writer.

5. Discuss what you are going to do after your agent calls and tells you she has sold your book?

6. What would you do if you could not write?

7. Pick a book that has changed your life and explain how.

8. What is the hardest part of writing?

9. What makes a writer successful?

10. What makes a writer a failure?

About the Author

Scott P. Craig has been a copywriter for his own business and has written everything from sales letters to resumes. He took his passion for writing with him to his current endeavor, teaching. He works with America's future each day and uses many of the prompts in here to inspire his students to write freely.